Collected Poems 2
2000 - 16

Jamie Inglis

© PROHIBITED PUBLICATIONS
MMXX

collected poems 2 2000-16

© Jamie Inglis 2020. All rights reserved.
Paperback First Edition October 2020.
ISBN 978-1-9163542-1-0

Many thanks to Jim Dalziel for kind permission to reproduce the
'Milestone Icon', 'Serious Birthday Card', 'King of the Mountains',
'Downfall of the Stand-up Comic', 'Montage' and
'Men with Walkmen returning Videos'.
Many thanks to Alex Nisbet for kind permission to reproduce
'Between the Lines', a mirror image of 'Time in Motion',
'Lilies, Edinburgh' and 'Burning the Page #1'.

Hubble image and satellite images © NASA/JPL.
Other satellite images © Google.
All photographs and other images © Jamie Inglis 2020.

New Neologisms - new words for new times   newneologisms.com
The Disorganised Society - real life is disorganised   disorganised.org
Burning the Page - from Paper to Pixel   burningthepage.com
The Science Fiction Index - The best of all time   sci-fi-index.com

Created with Lulu

Published by
PROHIBITED PUBLICATIONS
79 Bruntsfield Place
Edinburgh
EHIO 4HG
Scotland
www.prohibitedpublications.com

9 781916 354210

also by jamie inglis

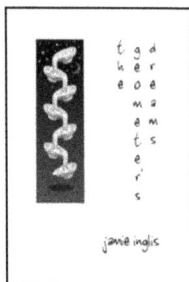

the geometer's dreams
(1992)

fractals & mnemonics
(1996)

hold on
(2000)

gluon notes
(2006)

experience engines
(2010)

Discovered Roads
(2018)

Warning

Do **not** look inside
Do **not** turn this page
Do **not** go any further

Do **not** stop now
Do **not** look up
Do **not** listen further

Do **not** speak
Do **not** ask
Do **not** question

Do **not** see
Do **not** imagine
Do **not** understand

Do **not** think
Do **not** wonder
Do **not** refuse

Do **not** turn
Do **not** worry
Do **not** change

Do **not** stand
Do **not act**
Do **not** move

Do **not** look
Do **not** listen

Do **not** do this
Do **not** do that
Do **not** now stop

Do **not** do
Do **not**hing

Do **not** do anything
Do **not** do now
Do **not** do nothing

Contents

gluon notes

jamie inglis

Contents *gluon notes*

Cont.

3

Contents cont.

some new notes

Montage © Jim Dalziel

Gluon Note

Give me time
and I will take you anywhere.
Give me a second
and I will take you to a star.

Give me time
and I will make you anywhere.
Give me a lifetime
and I will make you a star.

Gluon
There are eight different types of gluon: they have no mass,
travel at the speed of light and have colour and anti-colour.
Their behaviour is described by the theory of quantum chromodynamics.
Oxford Paperback Encyclopaedia, © Oxford University Press 1998

Dream night

Maybe tonight
is a dream night
something to remember, for tomorrow.

Maybe tonight
is a silent night
nothing to remember, if this is tomorrow.

Maybe tonight
is another night
everything remembered, it is tomorrow.

Warriors of Xian

Acres of soldiers
arrayed in square fields
standing, made from clay.

Cavalrymen and horses
eerily silent
in the red earth.

A motionless army
still for centuries
waiting the millennia away.

A tomb of terracotta,
legions of patient warriors
waiting through eternity.

Warriors of Xian
guarding forever
The Emperor's future.

For Boa Ninh   (2)

Wait for me here
until forever.

Wait for me here
until after forever.

Wait for me here
until forever has passed.

Wait for me here
make me be here.

Wreath Street, Hanoi 1994

The next mark

Every thought anew
a marker of mortality.
Acquired in life's footsteps,
as the history unwinds.

What treadmarks of fate
continue to wait.
Each ready to print
the next unseen mark.

9/11 2000

The days of the Nations are almost past.

A last few struggle to a bloody independence
as the Balkans, the Caucuses and Palestine
wade through their bloody births.

The US attempts to subdue the world
with Coke and MacDonald's
whilst policing the rest.

In response Islam gathers strength
and sometime not far from now
only madness will save the rest.

After the bomb

Pools of hard liquid darkness glitter
shining black reflections from furnace light.
An eerie spitting glow of retreating heat
cooling and cracking after the suns fire.
A moments inferno of neutrino streams
melting peace, melting all in this world.

Blasted, jagged, flattened, torn cityscape
plutonium powder, dusting death around.
Covering structures, remnant shards
deposited surfactant of staggering roentgens.

Only rubbled remains of megatonage force
flattened fields of every city street.
Flowing tarmac stopped in mid wave
multiple sulking naked industrial skeletons.

Total silence of event aftermath
concentrated quiet of singularity event.
Utter peace from life's complete absence,
desolating epicentre sterilises microbes upwards.
Every human a powdered shadow
imprinted forever in that instant fire.

Walking In Soldiers Footsteps

Walking in soldiers footsteps.
Battling again their fights.
Long-over and forgotten footsteps.
That lead to death for another right.

Walking in soldiers footsteps.
Descending into their night.
No-one can make them alive again.
Did they die in glory, or in vain?

Walking in soldiers footsteps.
Living again through their days.
Memories, remembered now without blame,
a candlelight for the eternal flame.

Saint-Nazaire

Order of Battle

(MGB 314)

(ML 270) (torpedo) **7**
Irwin

8 (ML 169) (torpedo)
Boyd

H.M.S. Campbeltown

GROUP ONE
to land at Old Mole

GROUP TWO
to land in Old Entrance

(ML 447) **9**
Platt, with Birney's
assault party for Old Mole

1 (ML 192)
Stephens, with Burn's assault party

(ML 341) **10**
Briault, with Hodgson's assault party;
Transferred to No.15

2 (ML 262)
Burt, with Woodcock (demolition)
And Morgan (Protection)

(ML 457) **11**
Collier, with Pritchard,
Walton and Watson

3 (ML 267)
Beart, with Moss's h.q. party

(ML 307) **12**
Wallis, with Bradley (demolition)

4 (ML 268)
Tillie, with Pennington (demolition)
And Jenkins (Protection)

(ML 443) **13**
Horlock, with Wilson,
Bassett-Wilson and Bonvin (demolition)
and Houghton (Protection)

5 (ML 156) (torpedo)
Fenton, with Hooper's assault party

(ML 306) **14**
Henderson, with Swayne (demolition)
And Houghton (Protection)

6 (ML 177) (torpedo)
Rodier, with Haines's assault party

(ML 446) **15**
Falconer; took over from No. 10

16 (ML 298)
Beck; spare

17 (MTB 74)
Wynn

The Greatest Raid of All

TGV Atlantique.
Taking the bullet to Saint-Nazaire
to meet the men who came ashore
in The Greatest Raid of All.

Six hundred men
do battle for a little over thirty minutes.
Five are awarded the Victoria Cross
in The Greatest Raid of All.

Almost forgotten now
that seventy years have passed.
Remember the (m) now
in The Greatest Raid of All.

On the way

Eighteen months after the Battle of Britain
the war was at its bleakest.
So the assault on Europe began
with six hundred Commandos attacking Saint-Nazaire.

Going back to where they landed
with their friends and comrades.
Thirty minutes for them and seventy years on.
Thirty minutes for me, just time to make tea.

The Charioteers

Walking in valiant footsteps
brave men stepping out ahead.
Stepping out onto the quay
for the hour of all their lives.

Walking in valiant footsteps
brave Charioteers arriving on the battleground.
Heading off to their objectives
for the final hour of many lives.

Heading for the quay

Heading for Saint-Nazaire harbour in small boats.
Naked under the night sky
and to the defenders waiting ashore.

I will be working late this night
as the dead and wounded appear
at my quayside site for the operation.

Submarine pens. Seventy years later

Submarine pens

Silent and sulking
the submarine pens
sit brooding over the dock.
Solid concrete seventy years on
still impregnable
still sombre
sometime tourist attraction.
Ghosts of U-Boats long gone.
Some reminders
stay forever.

Cimetiere Britannique

Behind Pornichet
Cimetiere Britannique

From Southampton to Saint-Nazaire
then silent suburban rows
hidden behind Pornichet.

Neat white rows of all the men
who fell that day
in The Greatest Raid of All.

No signs and little mention
of their bravery that day
hidden behind Pornichet.

Neat white rows
one marked by a cross of poppies
from a recent visitor.

A white marble circle
marks the entrance
to this little plot of (Great) Britain.

Almost forgotten now
only seventy years or so later
hidden behind Pornichet.

Monument des Morts

Monument des Commandos

Armistice morning, Saint-Nazaire 11.11.00

At eleven 'o' clock
the old men wearing their medals
and the standard bearers and the band
gather with fanfare
at the monument des morts.

More medals are presented.
Brave speeches are made
to remember those who are dead.

The wreaths are laid.
The standards are lowered
and a hundred doves take to the air.

The band form up
and the old soldiers behind
march off with their memories.

One hundred yards down the quayside
the Monument des Commandos is quiet
no flags, no ceremony today.

Valour

Looking for moments.
A resonance
from the stream
that guides our hearts.

Moments of men.
The resonance of their valour
clear in our hearts.
Never, from here to depart.

after September 11th

New York 9/12

Virtual war poems

Still reporting live
on the first 21st century war.
The Terror War.
From a frontline living room,
somewhere near you.

26

A new act of warfare

Terror from the air
a new act of warfare.

Terror from the air
now it could be anywhere.

Terror from the air
will now always be there.

Terror from the air
will lead us nowhere.

A Hole in the Heart of New York

Lost soul in New York.
Lost innocence in New York.

After the war started
the bodies were removed for weeks.
Then more than a month.
There was a hole in the heart of New York
with mangled bodies emerging one by one.
Into the light for the world to see.
Terror at the heart of New York.
Starting a war on terror
leading to holes in all our hearts.

The Three Minute War

The first war to start
with a three minute silence.
How long will the silences be
when this war is over?

Three minute war
delivered as infobytes
of three minutes of war
as we watch in silence.

The three minute war.
But which three minutes
will hold the truth
and seal our future as fate?

11am, 04.10.01
Three minute silence on flight to London

A Year of Rubble

After the first hour
of the first war
of the twenty-first century.

There was a year
of rubble and bodies
from the first hour of the terror war.

After the first hour
of the first move
there were pieces all over the world.

After the first hour
we could stand no more
and the waiting started
for the end of the war.

War Day Three

War Day Three
and now years of war lie ahead.
Only the tears of Allah
and all his followers
will satisfy the US.

War Day Three
more countries at war lie ahead.
Collapsing and imploding
till Islam is revealed
will satisfy the US.

War Day Three
deaths every day in the war ahead.
Only the tears of Allah
and all his followers
will satisfy the US.

Six weeks in

Six weeks in
and the site of ground zero
continues to smoulder.

Six weeks in
the IRA give up the gun
and peace begins to come.

Six weeks in
cannabis now scores a C
and its OK to smoke, man.

Six weeks in
least news of the war today
from those making War on Terror.

Six weeks in
first pictures of Taliban soldiers
in caves in the mountains.

Six weeks in
the West begins to wonder
are we ready for the stone age with guns.

Mazar-i-Sharif

Mazar-i-Sharif.
Massacre
of men and infidels.

The first American
Johnny Span
from the CIA.

Hundreds of Taliban
ready to die
for Islam.

Mazar-i-Sharif
massacre
no-one survives.

Mazar-i-Sharif
memories
will never sleep.

Five years on
12th September 2006

Five years on
the war on terror goes on.
Five years on
the war goes on and on.
Five years on
how long will this go on?
Five years on
who knows when this will stop?
Five years on
who knows how this will end?

some more new

Downfall of the Stand Up Comic © Jim Dalziel

Warm Rain

The lights are the warm rain
of an ever beckoning fame.

The lights are the warm rain
of the pressure of photons.
Washing away everyone's pain,
highlighting even a tiny stain.
Asking always,
for a last refrain.

Speaking as friends

Speak to me as a friend
and treat me as someone you have just met.

We should have no secrets
and your body should tell me no lies.

Tell me only your truest thoughts
that only a stranger should ever hear.

Red September   (Game Plan)

It is September of the year 2031.
An enormous army of soldierbots
pour outwards from China
in Operation Red September.

By September 2031 China
is producing one million soldierbots a day
in a plan to dominate the world
codename Red September.

Throughout September 2031 the soldierbots advance
conquering all the world before them.
Only you, stand in the way
of Red September.

Mr nothing to do with me

Mr nothing to do with me
he's so sad to see.

He can't help but lie
its so easy to see.

Mr nothing to do with me
he's a slob of the first degree.

What could he wish to be
Mr nothing to do with me.

Rich, famous and on tv
he would (be the first to) no doubt agree.

Dream on, Mr nothing to do with me

abc

abc
I see your love for me
one face in three.

abc
Do you see what I see
when you look at me?

abc
I see your face in me
setting us free.

Saving Face
One letter for a Chinese Compromise

Bao Chi   very sorry   很抱歉

Dao Chi   very sorry, partly at fault   保持

Scottish Haiku's

Nihilist Credo

Whatever comes next
comes next.
Come whatever, next
comes next.

Whatever comes next,
next whatever.
Come whatever
next comes.

The Pacifists Credo
or Give then Guns

If they want to fight,
  give them guns.

To let them finish,
  every war in sight.

Always tomorrow

Knowing you will never grow old
what would it mean to you?

How would you hold forever in your hands
making sense of always having tomorrow.

Gene haiku

Your genes are your memories.

They are all that remember you.

more New Neologisms

www.NewNeologisms.com

INFO*Gale*

A googolplex of information searched every day,
a blizzard of information received every day.

A knowledge hurricane coming this way,
page upon page of information blowing us away.

www.infogale.com

ChaosHOT

Quantum foam boiling, tearing order apart,
unforeseen event strings, appear at every turn.

Quantum foam steaming, order fails to start,
chaotic event strings, life begins to burn.

www.chaoshot.com

DoNoTime

Time and place, here and now,
structure and style, rules if you want.

Form and function, content and design,
structure and style, rules if you need.

www.donotime.com

TimePits

Forever holes in the space time continuum,
frozen moments sleeping through eternity.

Forever traps in the space time continuum,
locked and awaiting the end of eternity.

www.timepits.com

LoGicDaY

Today everything will go exactly to plan,
that is the logic since time began.

Today will be nothing that is not planned,
that was the logic when today began.

www.logicday.com

NoLeaders

If you lead, you will be followed.

If you follow, you will be led.

www.noleaders.com

colophon

Take it slowly

Take it slowly
see the story.

Take it slowly
see the story
unfold before you.

Take it slowly
see the story.
      Its you.

experience
engines

jamie inglis

Contents *experience engines*

Cont.

Start Engines

The page that was never there

You won't find it here.
You won't find it there.
The page is everywhere.

You won't find it here.
You won't find it anywhere.
Your page is everywhere.

You won't find it here.
You'll never find it now.
The page was never there.

A Thread Understood
'Pattern Recognition'

A pattern brought to life
before your blinkered eyes.

A pattern exposed to light
the ideas shining ever brighter.

A thread unravelled
to be better understood.

A thread understood
a threat laid to rest.

The Pointless Club

All the streets are numbered there,
somewhere between heaven and here.
Long passageways full of secret keys.
A lost island locked in the trees.

All the avenues are numbered there,
some oasis that we all share.
Beyond the maze that is despair,
life's utopia for all to compare.

All the roads are numbered there,
somewhere between heaven and here.
Many crossroads full of hidden signs,
our island, always our times.

A life of dreams

We live a life of dreams.
Dreams of ourselves, dreams of others.

A life full of dreams.
Dreams of people, dreams of places.

A full life of dreams.
Dreamed by ourselves, not by others.

You are my world

You are my world,
all of it, and nothing less.

You are all my world,
all of you, and nothing less.

You will be my world,
all of time, and nothing less.

Do not save the best for last

Do not save the best for last.
Now is the best.

Do not ask
how long will it last?

Longer than this moment
has taken to pass.

Hot and Cold Conundrum

Hot taps on the left, cold taps on the right.
No, cold on the left, hot on the right.
No, that can't be right,
cold is on the right.

There must be a rule to get it right
but is it hot or cold on the right.

Select Society 2

Deselected from The Select Society.
Standing outside The Inner Circle.
Reselected for The Select Society.
Stepping inside The Inner Circle.

Life in and out of Lots of Societies.
Inside and out of All the Circles.
Death inside Some of these Societies.
Stuck within One of the Circles.

Faith in You

Do not put your faith in one belief.
Do not put your faith in one religion.
Do not put your faith in one belief system.

Do not put your faith in one belief.
Do not put your faith in world peace.
Do not put your faith in human nature.

Put your faith in your belief.
Put your faith in your conviction.
Put your faith in you.

Living long enough to understand locks

Locks on our doors,
locks on our secrets,
all of us prone to deceit.

Doubts of our security,
doubts of our exposure,
all of us prone to doubt.

Some doors are secure,
some secrets are safe,
all of us prone to doubt.

Living long enough to understand,
locks are always open,
with those you truly trust.

It's easy to remember

Love at first sight
it's easy to remember.
I did not put up a fight
it's easy to remember.

Love at first sight
it's easy to remember.
It was now and right
it's easy to remember.

Love at first sight
it's easy to remember.
Lying awake through the night
it's easy to remember.

Love at first sight
it's easy to remember.
Forever in my sight
no need to remember.

Travel Notes

Isla de Ometepe, Lago de Nicaragua

The Lost Half Hour
Flying to Canada and back

London to St. John's,
  four hours back.

St. John's to Halifax,
  a half hour back.

Halifax to London,
  four hours forward.

That lost half hour,
  where is it now?

Titanic Cemetery, Halifax, Nova Scotia

Touching the Fire Dragon

Perched on the caldera's rim.
A rumble builds beneath your feet
and blows the explosion through your soles.
Add deafening sound and the caldera erupts.
Throwing tons of lava and rocks towards the clouds.
A molten vertical river rising before your eyes
and turning and raining back down below your feet.
A searing red retinal streak.
Touched, the Fire Dragon.

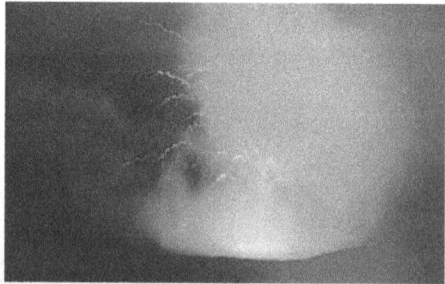

Mount Yasur, Tanna Island, Vanuatu (2005)

Mr CIA Man on the ferry to New Amsterdam

New Amsterdam ferry with Mr CIA.
A lie from the first about crossing from Suriname.

Investigating murders in these here parts.
Superintendent killed was it that?
New York City cop now working for Justice.
A reconnaissance of possible hostile.
We're on holiday no knowledge of murders.
From Scotland, not Irish and IRA.

The ferry started loading, Mr CIA to his armour.
Only gates were opening still time to wonder.
No cars were moving yet Mr CIA.
Only people from everywhere crossing over today.

Mr CIA doesn't know the length of the crossing.
I speak politely to people passing. Thirty minutes.
Going back to speak to Mr CIA alarms the spooks.
Set Mr CIA on edge for thirty entertaining minutes.

Cont.

Cont.

An unknown quantity relaxing and smoking on the ferry.
To New Amsterdam with Mr CIA.
With armoured 4x4, partner and locals.
Still not Irish, no thanks to a Guinness.
Water on the ferry to New Amsterdam courtesy of Mr CIA.
Happy to banter with locals, joking and in your face.

Wary of inconsistencies is the unknown stranger.
Watching Mr CIA wonder on the ferry to New Amsterdam.

As you travel more

As you travel more.
More cities, lands and people
are part of your world
and are devastated in your wake
or they are preparing for their own storm.

As you travel more.
You become sensitised to the world's disasters.
A tsunami here, a bomb there,
a hurricane somewhere else,
a terrorist attack again.

In an age of global media
for most a faraway disaster.
No connectedness, to events unfolding.
For those caught up, each disaster is personal.

As you travel more,
in our time of disaster and terror.
The cities, lands and people
are changing and uniting,
and these voices will be heard.

Los Almendros de San Lorenzo
(not the only gays in the village)

Los Almendros de San Lorenzo
made a fine mojito, the best in Suchitoto.
A gay Parisian boutique hotel in Suchitoto,
the poorer lover manages the business.
Now a big new hotel overlooking the square
a gay Spaniard runs with his secret
Salvadorian business lover.
Frisson for the only gay loses its savour.
Suchitoto now has a gay community
always at each other's throats.
The flavour of unique has been lost to normality.
The new gays take their profit
and retire to the coast.
Parisian and partner left behind.

The Beach at Waikiki

Walking the beach at Waikiki.
Diamond Head brooding at our back.
Browning bodies bake prone on the sand
waves roll through thousands in the sea.
Foaming at the waterline, a scum of factor
reflecting oil slicks on the surface of the sea.
Through a sinking sunset watched
mostly by silent American and Japanese eyes
from countless cocktail bars and grills.
The towering concrete of rooms and suites behind
encasing the dream of the beach at Waikiki.

In Paris, waiting for the tour

In Paris, waiting for the tour to arrive.
Preparing for the peleton
or the breakaway on the Champs-Elysee.
Glory before the Arc in a couple of days.

In Paris, two days before the tour.
A Friday, the holidays start today.
By Monday, all of Paris will be away.
On Sunday, all stand to hail the tour.

King of the Mountains © Jim Dalziel

from a frontline living room

Saddam in their sights

How many more nights
of Saddam in their sights
before somebody blinks
and out go the lights.

Second attack inevitable

20.05.02
Six months into The War on Terror
the US warns a Second attack is inevitable.

The next attack is coming.
Al-Qaeda are preparing
their second attack.

This war is far from over.
This war is far from won.

One attack behind us.
How many more to come?

Wednesday 29th May 2002

Wednesday 29th May 2002.
Last day of clearing-up Ground Zero.
Last piece of wreckage removed.
Last steel girder cut down
wrapped in a shroud
and borne aloft
to leave Ground Zero
and the final ceremony tomorrow.

11 Months After

Now forty US soldiers dead
11 months after 9/11.

Hundreds or thousands of Afghan dead
11 months after 9/11.

Hundreds or thousands more around the world
11 months after 9/11.

Hundreds or thousands or many more to die
In The War on Terror after 9/11.

10/12 Bali

Bombs explode
fifteen and twenty years in my past
and resonate through the years.

Bombs in paradise
not as I remember it
but in a western theme park paradise.

Bombs in western paradise
the second front of dreaded terror.
Next Disneyland and Uncle Sam.

Bombs on 9/11, 10/12.
The anniversaries begin to coincide
in a forever war for both sides.

Gulf War II

On the brink
of Gulf War II.
This month, March
they say for sure.

On the brink
of a war without frontiers.
This month, forever
our world will change.

A Minute to Midnight

A minute to midnight
to invade Iraq.

A minute to midnight
how will they fight back.

A minute to midnight
why do we attack?

A minute to midnight
Invasion Iraq.

A minute to midnight
not to late to turn back.

A minute to midnight
and the start of the flack.

A minute to midnight
standby Iraq.

A minute to midnight
Goodbye Iraq.

Five years on
12th September 2006

Five years on, year one,
The War on Terror goes on.

Five years on, year two,
The War goes on and on.

Five years on, year three,
how long will this go on?

Five years on, year four,
who knows when this will stop?

Five years on, year five and counting,
who knows how this will end?

Las Malvinas War Memorial, Buenos Aires 2008

Argentinian 50 Peso note, introduced 2015

The last war we fought on our own

Twenty-five years after Gotcha
modest remembrance of the end of empire.
One thousand deaths in a short war
for our Falkland Overseas Territories.

Twenty-five years after the Belgrano,
Sheffield, Sir Galahad, Atlantic Conveyer and more.
To watery graves in the South Atlantic
and barren hillside graves, in the South Atlantic.

Twenty-five years after hostilities
only we and Argentina remember.
Would we act the same today
for our Falkland Overseas Territories?

April 2007

Tomorrow

Ta Prohm, Siam Reap, Cambodia

When the final night falls

To be with you
when the stars fall.

To be with you
when the stars fall from the sky.

To be with you
when the last night falls.

To be with you
when darkness falls.

To be with you
when the final night falls.

Fast Anaesthetisers

Hard to say, easy to not notice.
Those fast aneasthetisers
we meet every day.

Fast aneasthetisers, from TV to soap.
Infoporn on the infobhan
pervading our lives.

Fast aneasthetisers, go digital at night.
Pixels and gigabytes
capturing our lives.

Fractal String

Bloodhound String
kernal 386.exe

Live the world
Be the world
Live the web
Worldweb
Join the world
Join the worldweb
Run the world
Who runs the web
Whose in charge
Whose in charge here
No-one's in charge
No-one's in charge now
We run the world
This is how the world runs
This is how the web runs
This is how the web works
We fix your organisation
We run the worldweb
We run the web
We run the world

Poem for Search Engines
[128 bit unencrypted poem]

Poem, poem, poem, poem.
Poem, poem, poem, poem.

Poem, poem, poem, poem.
Poem, poem, poem, poem.

Poem, poem, poem, poem.
Poem, poem, poem, poem.

Poem, poem, poem, poem.
Poem, poem, poem, poem.

01110000 01101111 01100101 01101101
01110000 01101111 01100101 01101101
01110000 01101111 01100101 01101101
01110000 01101111 01100101 01101101

01110000 01101111 01100101 01101101
01110000 01101111 01100101 01101101
01110000 01101111 01100101 01101101
01110000 01101111 01100101 01101101

The C Library

If disaster strikes
and there are no more books
at least you will have
those you own.

If disaster strikes again
and books are to valuable to be lent
only your own to read again.
Not with a Classics Library.

I will be me again

I will be me again
no matter what they take.
I will be I again
whatever I should lose.

It will still be me
after their damage is done.
It will still be I
when loss has turned to gain.

One event

Now, in our time
one event
can change the world in a day.

Throughout time
one event
could change your world in a day.

Before our time
one event
could not change the world in a day.

Anytime now
one event
could change the world in a day.

In our time
one event
will change the world in a day.

VCR Dementia

Blank technology spots
Areas of electronic darkness
Gaps of information understanding
Data loss on the highway
Missing facets of function
Advancing areas of noise
Blank knowledge spots
Blank spots
Blank

Men with Walkmen returning videos © Jim Dalziel

Future History

Strong common history
binds our lives together.
Mirror image roots
shaped throughout our childhood.

Early years encircling
ties our current life.
Shared years of growing
towards our common future.

Large Hadron Collider

Hadrons collide at the start of time.
From nothing, something leads to everything.

Looking at light from the dawn of time.
Nothing familiar in the Ultra Deep Field.

Hubble Ultra Deep Field © NASA/JPL

Emergent Functions

The mathematics of Emergent Functions.
Space outwith our own geometry's.
Worlds without number at every junction.
Life unique in all these universes.

We are the Emergent Function.

Master of the Universe, Sir Eduardo Paolozzi,
Dean Gallery, Edinburgh

New Scottish Politics

MSP's Offices, Scottish Parliament, Edinburgh

Three men, two dead to blame

A Scottish Parliament is built
[Three men, two dead to blame].

The architect - Enric Miralles
for designing such an expensive building.

The First Minister - Donald Dewar
for approving the building.

The Presiding Officer - Lord [call me Sir David] Steel
for dithering about the building.

(Cost £500 Million. Ten times the estimate.)

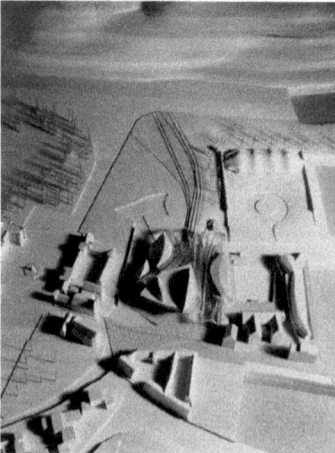

First model

One week away

In the week we were away
The Scottish Parliament became
what it was always destined to be
the very finest operatic comedie.

A Lord MSP sets fire to curtains.
The Scottish Socialists expel their founder.
What further entertainment awaits us?
A bargain at £500 million pounds.

Our first constitutional crisis

One month after the historic Scots election
our first constitutional crisis appears.
A memorandum in a tent with the Libyan dictator
has Scotland's First Minister the happiest in years.

The 10% Democracy?

The 20% Democracy.
What led us here?
50% of people vote,
40% of these elect a Government,
equals 20% of the population.
80% voted for someone else
    or not at all.
National Governments no longer represent.
Local Councils are already at 15% Democracy.
In another ten years.
The 10% Democracy?

Edinburgh's G8 moment

And yet, somehow now
the world turns and watches
Edinburgh, Scotland
awaiting its G8 moment.

Dreams of Enlightenment days past.
Dreams of poverty in the past.
Nightmares of the world unlocked at last.

And yes, this is now
our moment has come at last.
All our voices will be heard
filling the G8 moment.

And yes, our now
will be with the world watching.
Turning our dreams to dust or light.
And you? In your G8 moment.

Wha's for a dram?

Give me a splash
in the bottom of the glass.
No, that can't be right
it doesn't rhyme.

Give me a dash
in the bottom of the glass.
No, not right either
still doesn't rhyme.

Give me a dram
that's Scotland's dwam.

Scottish Haiku's

White Peacock, Funchal Botanical Gardens, Madeira

Knowledge Haiku

Walking in new directions
with no knowledge of before.

Walking in different directions
before the knowledge goes.

Haiku for Lonely Planet

For some it is the travel path.
For others it is the aftermath.

The Complete Citizen

50% Socialist, of course.
25% Nationalist, naturally.
25% Anarchist, who me?

Where in time

Time is also a where.
Now is somewhere in time.

This where in time
is now.

Only memories are left
as dreams of then.

Waiting Game

Steady waiting game, to prevent your gain,
holding on, taking the strain.
Quarter, quatrain, it's only a game,
nothing ever stays the same.

RLS was wrong

Someone to love.
Someone who loves you.
Somewhere to belong.
Somewhere to hope for.

What lies ahead is already here

What's ahead of us
is here now.
If we could see
the sparks here and now,
the time ahead of us
would be visible now.

Hanging Dante, Prvic Luka, Croatia

The Human Quandary

The outward and inward urges.
Forever forward and beckoning back.

Drawing us on and back within.
Holding us hypnotised and promising us peace.

Concrete Hellfire

Religion is conviction without evidence.
Evidence is the religion of conviction.
Conviction is the evidence of religion.

Unexpected Life

Just because it happens
doesn't mean
you have to go looking for it.

Friendship Haiku

Friendship always (usually) survives honesty
but very rarely lies.

more

New Neologisms

	RunChaos
	TimeDart
	textexit
	E-Memes
	DoNoInfo
	EmitTime

www.NewNeologisms.com

RunChaos

Initiate each unstable event chain,
leading to chaos who knows when.

Initiate every unstable event chain,
leading to chaos here, there and everywhen.

www.runchaos.com

next

TimeDart

A pierced moment from the past,
flies through time designed to last.

A memory arrow from the past,
strikes through reality outwith our grasp.

www.timedart.com

next

textexit

Final words written saved and sent,
before your eyes and in your mind.

Final words written before getting bent,
adverts, clicks and sales pay the rent mind.

www.textexit.com

next

E-Memes

Electronic ideas spreading through cyberspace,
as a storm of microscopic motes.

Electronic ideas spreading through the human race,
inside a cloud of driven nanobots.

www.e-memes.com

next

EmitTime

Time backwards and time forward.
Backwards time and forward time.

Living within the flow of time.
Creating time from the mirror.

www.emittime.com

next

DoNoInfo

Avoiding information trails in data hungry devices, invisible steps at the machine interface.

Outside the information track
                    in memory hungry mainframes,
silent footsteps passing without leaving a trace.

www.DoNoInfo.com

Colophon

**End of the day poem
of the leftover words**

When you write a few words
and give them away
and send them on their way
they are lost forever
those words you wrote
that day.

Telendos, Greece

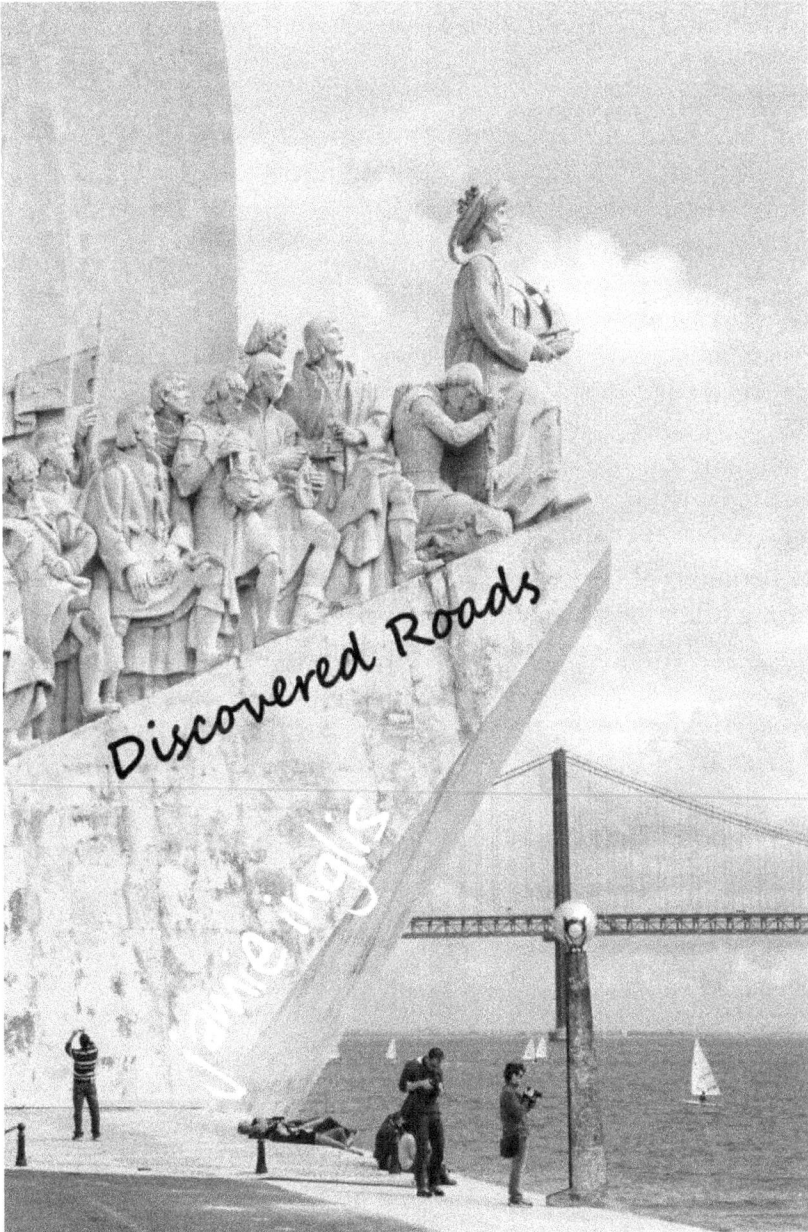

Discovered Roads

Jamie Inglis

Contents *Discovered Roads*

Cont.

Cont.

First Roads

Start Here / Intro

First starting to look.
No, I mean really look.
What can you see?
A few lines in front of you.
Stop, look around
what you really see
is all around you.
Just take the time to look.

Mothers of the Disappeared
outside the Presidential Palace, Buenos Aires (2008)

Mothers still waiting

Mothers still waiting
After years have passed
Still waiting
After decades have passed.

Mothers still waiting
For sons and daughters
Still waiting
For sisters and brothers.

Mothers still waiting
Circling the square
Still waiting
With photos of the disappeared.

Mothers still waiting
In hope not fear
Still waiting
For answers to appear.

Mothers still waiting
Fewer every year
Still waiting
For the truth to be clear.

Fred the Shed

Sir Fred the Shed
where are you now?
Our lives in shreds
come take a bow.

Sir Fred the Shed
no doubt in hiding now.
Our lives in debt,
to you we kowtow?

Sir Fred the Shed
the banker run out of town.
Our lives spent repaying
the wankers
who turned out to be clowns.

The Bonfire of the Banks

Great economic days
Great economic daze

Banks are reeling
Depositors are running
Shareholders are ruined

Banks are nationalised
Depositors are numb
Shareholders are still ruined

Banks are ours
Everyone loses but bankers
Taxpayers pick up the bill

Great economic haze
Great economic maze

08.10.08
Banks nationalised

© CNN

© Vatican TV

A Strong God Delusion Moment

The crescendo of The God Delusion
when a hundred elderly male cardinals
are cloistered for the Papal conclave.

The apex of The God Delusion
when no-one applies to be Pope
and God tells the others how to vote.

The fanfare of The God Delusion
when artificial white smoke appears
and a new Peter waves to the crowds.

Lightning on the Links

Deeper quiet after the storm
Lightning strikes then silence
Wave fronts passing outwards
Sonic cloud of mighty decibels
Structures shake at the storms heart
One moment, the storm has passed
Deeper silence after the storm

But the moment has not passed
A further flash of light
Crash then silence supersound

Lightning over Oradea, Romania © Mircea Madau

Travelled Roads

Jesuitic Mission of *Santisima Trinidad del Parana,*
Encarnation, Paraguay

Masters of Time

Masters of this moment
and the last one.
Masters of this moment
and the next one.

Masters of every moment
and of each one.
Masters of the first moment
and the last one.

Masters of our moment
and every other one.
Masters of your moment
and those to come.

Mesmerised by dreams

Mesmerised by the dreams that never materialised.
Waking to the dawn of what is real life.
Visions of a future devoid of the truth.
Memories now of what should have been.

Innocence lost with the intervals of time.
Fading aspirations with the failure of inspiration.
Evaporating hope of the heights of desire.
Memories now of what should have been.

Mesmerised by the dream that materialised.
Reminded always, that reality is man-made.
Singular choices shaping what lies ahead.
Memories now of what has been.

Cars Need Fuel

A lifetime watching the fuel gauge
Every cycle starting at full
Every drive reducing it further
Till the fuel gauge reaches the red zone
Then the fuel gauge is returned to full.

Repeat. Repeat. Repeat.
Repeat. Repeat. Repeat.
Repeat. Repeat. Repeat.
Repeat. Repeat. Repeat.
Repeat. Repeat. Repeat.
Repeat. Repeat. Repeat.

A lifetime of repeating the cycle
Cars need fuel
To get you from A to B
The price you pay
Goes up every day.

Dreams of Barak

A new face at the top of the table
promising change from the old world order.

A new hope at the dawn of depression
promising bailouts for everything bust.

A new vision for a new century
promising consensus as the only way ahead.

A new man we never thought we'd see
promising to be different for all the world to see.

A new man at the top of the world
promising all things are possible.

Later

Later, after the moment had passed
A voice whispered sweetly in my ear
Notions of distant memory and loss
Awakening a primitive, older fear.

Longer, after the moment has passed by
The voice growing fainter but still near
Suggests a forgotten time and moment
Illuminating a modern, timeless here.

Back-stories

Creating back-stories
in the photos of strangers.
Two people hidden from recognition
hands in front of faces.
Spotted in the later, and larger review.
Prompting the stranger
to create a back-story
for the two people
possibly hiding? from recognition.

Continuous Friends /
A Set of Lines

Paths crossing again.
Another moment
we meet again.

Paths crossing again.
Another moment
we meet again.

Paths cross again.
Continuous moments
as we meet again.

Paths recrossing again.
More moments
spent together again.

Paths crisscrossing again.
Fleeting moments
as we pass again.

Paths crossout again.
Missed moments
lost to us again.

Paths crossover again.
Discontinuous moments
till we meet again.

Flight Radar image 16.04.10
Northern Europe No fly zone 15 - 23 April 2010

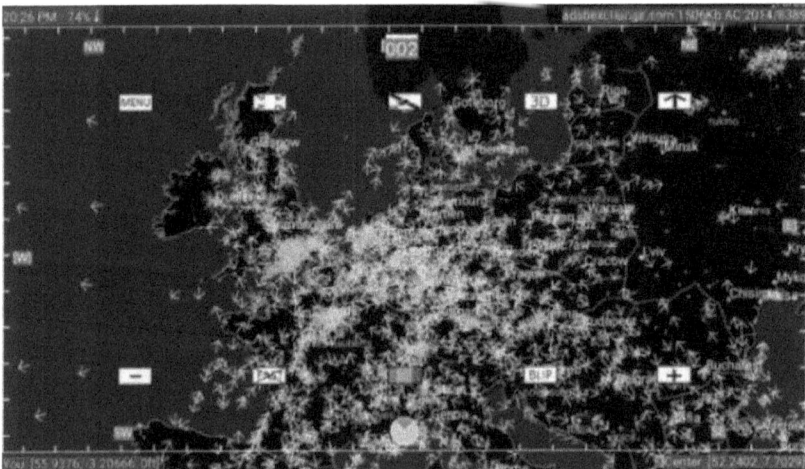

ADSB Air Traffic image, 16.06.18

Forty-eight hours of no fly

Not a cloud or a contrail to be seen,
the skies over Scotland
the bluest they've ever been.
Severe clear the pilots call it.

A volcano in Iceland clears the sky
not a single vapour trail up on high.
No movement through the sky,
only birds flying not very high
through a deserted azure sky.
Thanks to Iceland's dust up high
before our eyes a truly unique sky.

The end of New Labour 11.05.10

The era of New Labour ends today.
A statesman from Fife leaves with his children
and the new child from the old Tories,
with pregnant wife walks into the glare.

Thirteen years of New Labour ends today.
A new political landscape starts this day
and the new child of coalition(s)
will be the offspring of every future election day.

Decluttering

Lightening loads all and each of us carry.

Shelves, drawers, cupboards, cellars.
Yielding detritus, hoarding, memories and more.
Collected, accumulated, saved and hidden.

Everything taking up space and time.
Removing frees the space and mind,
to move on less weighted down.

Mona Lisa   [The Celebrity]

The world's first celebrity painting
surrounded by crowds snapping away.
I must warn you the next experience
always contains flash photography.

The world's first stationary celebrity.
Flickering constantly
behind a barrage of flashguns.
Crowds surrounding, swirling, closing-in
flashing, then moving away.
Every day the same experience
ten thousand digital images more.

The world's first unknown celebrity.
Countless strangers stopping for a few moments.
Press the button record the scene,
miss the experience.
That knowing smile,
suits us even more now.

The iterations of the day

The iterations of the day
The routines of our life
That we measure every day
And chart the passing of our life.

The iterations of the day
The subroutines we dance
So many times every day
And mark our passing in a trance.

The iterations of the day
The cycles turned another way
Each one different every day
Leaving a mark, who can say.

Mona Lisa Reality

Starting off in the wrong direction

Turning north away from the sun
and the mirrors of mortal vanity.
Bright lures of fascinating snares
corroding the hearts of those less wary.

Turning north away from the sun
footsteps avoiding the beaten path
and the baubles of broken mortality
corrupting the brains of those less wary.

Turning north away from the sun
into the darkness of increasing uncertainty
for fresh light beyond the decay
capturing the minds of those still wary.

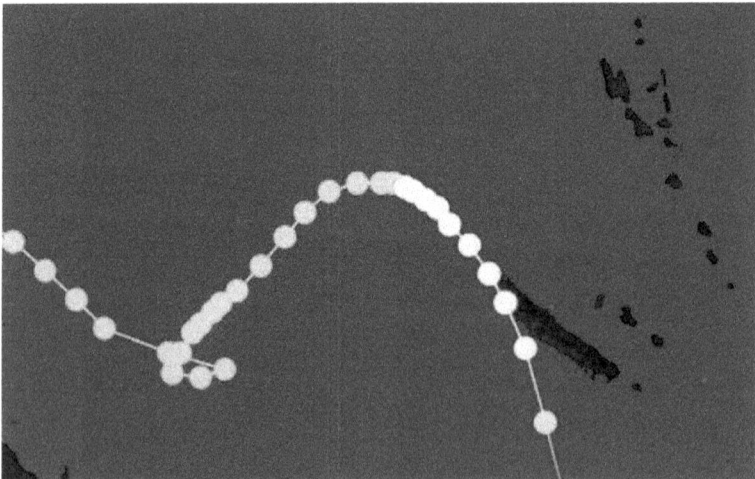

Severe Tropical Storm Freda (March 1982)

In the Eye

Standing in the eye of the hurricane
Standing in the eye of a monster storm
After the wind has done half its worst
The landscape flattened all around
Sudden Silence
The other side of the hurricane
The other side of the monster
Still to come
Nothing moves or makes a sound
Silence stretches on

A million photos of Pompeii

How many photos of Pompeii
are taken every day?

Twenty thousand visitors
on a busy day at Pompeii.

With digital cameras and phones
pointing every which way.

How many photos each of Pompeii
do they take in their one day?

At least fifty photos each
during their visit to Pompeii.

And a million 'new' photos of Pompeii
taken every single day, including today.

from a frontline living room

Iraq plus five

No end in sight
No sight of the end.

No sign of light
Around the next bend.

Five years of US might
A Hegemony to defend.

Neutrals taking flight
No-one left to tend.

Bombings a daily sight
(and) funerals to attend.

Soldiers patrol the night
Civilians left to fend.

Baghdad a building site
No-one left to mend.

No end in sight
No sight of the end.

23.01.08
Iraq War 5 years on   DoD – 'no end in sight'

143

02.19AM GMT 20/03/08

Five years after Shock and Awe
the US inhabits a wound still raw.

Five years after the invasion of Iraq
everyone's still waiting for the soldiers to come back.

Five years after the terrorists arrived
more fear and terror and deaths have been contrived.

Five years after the dictator was deposed
no WMD or terror links have been exposed.

Five years after the casualties started
no-one knows how many have departed.

Five years into an illegal war
strong hearts needed to heal the scar.

Five years in and no end in sight
whoever thought this was right?

20.03.08 5th anniversary Iraq invasion
9.19PM 19/03 US, 2.19AM 20/03 UK, 5.19AM 20/03 Baghdad

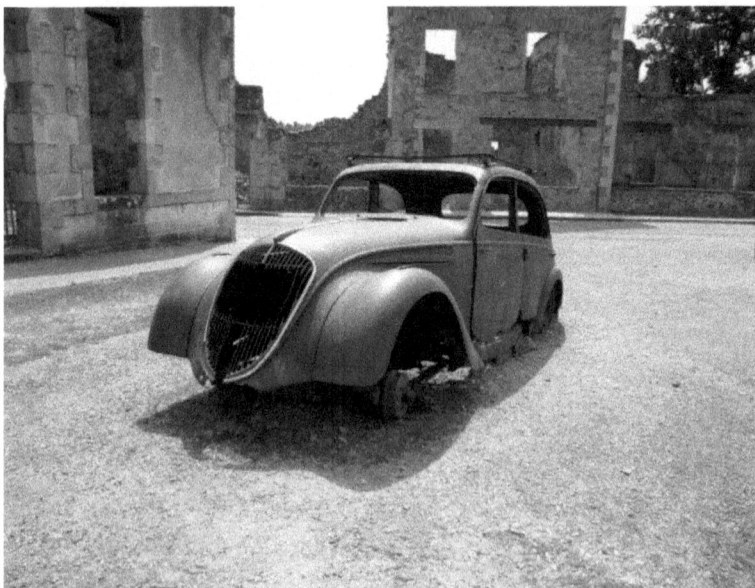

Oradour-sur-Glane, France (2009)

Oradour-sur-Glane
10th June 1944

Sunny Saturday afternoon.
A modern circle of iron seals the city.
Only entry through the Centre Memoire
past an exhibition to another massacre.

Silence in the City Martyre
for 642 people silenced in a day.
Blackened, shells of buildings line the street.
Dr. Jacques Desourteaux's burnt out car
the only object still on the street.

A church, without worshippers.
Full of murmuring respectful voices
eyes turning up to the open sky above.

An hour passes and the town becomes history.
Only a memory of the massacre remains today.
Respect and remembrance
the purpose of the day.

Bringing all the bodies home

Now we bring all our soldiers home
No more corner of a foreign field
Planted forever with fallen military men.

All the coffins come home
One or more at a time
Through a silent parade
To their home town.

Now we bring all the bodies home
No more hidden in foreign fields
Every death seen
one too many.

© PA

Ten years on

The wars in Afghanistan and Iraq
are still going on
but only two more years
until we move on.

Still soldiers on the frontline
wherever that is.
And now we have Syria
to add to the (our) list.

The War on Terror, which left long ago
is now against the Jihadists
and all of their friends
and they have the time.

After a failed foreign adventure
all we leave behind
are the markers for those
with no more time.

Trident

A nuclear relic from the cold war
that no-one needs any more.

A weapon of last and first resort
to fire back after or before
the nuclear holocaust that is no more.

Bombs come in backpacks and briefcases now
and individual soldiers who know they will die.

Our new Ironclads are pie in the sky.
A last resort relic to throw overboard.

Social Media Cul-de-sacs

Rembrandt's *The Night Watch*
The Reichsmuseum, Amsterdam

Poem for Facebook ™
[no time for poetry]

Everyone is too busy for poetry these days,
hours online on Facebook™ accounts.

What are you doing today, tomorrow, next day?
Spending hours on Facebook™ mounts.

No time for poetry in networked days,
updating Facebook™ is all that counts.

Poem for Facebook ™ V2.0
[no time for poetry]

Everyone is busy writing these days.
Hours online on Facebook™ accounts.

What you are doing and thinking every day.
Hours spent on Facebook™ inexorably mounts.

New time for poetry in networked days,
but updating Facebook™ is not what counts.

Try not to poke me after I'm gone.
23.02.10

The Night Watch 3D
Rembrandtplein (Rembrandt Square) Amsterdam
153

Twitter™ Poem

Look at what I'm doing now	26	
		1
Look what I'm doing now	23	
		1
Look what I'm doing now	23	
		1
Look what I'm doing now	23	
	98	
		1
Look what I'm doing now	23	
	122	
		1
Look what I'm doin	17	
	140	

Shake that shiny hand,

get in the picture

Twitter ™ Poem 2

Look at what I'm doing now   26
                                        1
What I'm doing now is important   31
                                        1
It's important you know what I'm doing now   41
                                        1
                                      101
Look again at what I'm doing now   33
                                      134

Twitter™ Poem 2A

Look at what I'm thinking now.   30
                                        1
What I'm thinking now is important.   35
                                        1
It's important you know what I'm thinking now.   45
                                        1
                                      113
Look again at what I'm thin   27
                                      140

Twitter™ Poem 3

	14		
		1	
Read what I write.	18		
		1	
Hear what I think.	18		
		1	
Know what I'm doing.	19		
			73
		1	
		1	
Read what I write.	18		
		1	
More than I think.	18		
		1	
Next thing I'm doing	20		
			133
		1	
T - Off.	6		
			140

Twitter™ Poem 3B

15

[Look at what I'm doing now!]

1

Read what I say.   16

1

Hear what I think.   17

1

Waste your time.   16

1

Tweet Off.   10

77

twits *n(OED 2017 Revised)* A person who uses Twitter™.

Last Seen on CCTV

Last grainy moments captured by chance.
On cameras in the corner
and by walls and poles that have eyes.

In the shops and on the streets
of our daily lives.

Trawled for our last images
before we could say
Goodbye.

Catching-up

Everyone's catching-up now.
Catching-up on their emails
their Facebook™ friends
their Twitter™ feeds
the TV they've missed.

Catching-up on what
while they have been offline?
Spam, posts, likes, tweets and retweets
that have passed
in the blink of an eye.

Everyone's catching-up on screens
held before their eyes.
Trying to catch-up
with a time already past
and (?now) slipping away fast.

Immersed in a Virtual Environment

From Texts to Streetview™
From Phone to Facebook™
From guide to TripAdvisor™

Living a Second Hand Life
Viewed through another's lens
the lens of others
the lens of another

From Postcards to Blogs
From eMails to Skype™
From Photos to Flikr™

An ever more virtual life
Perceived through the layers of others

From Reality to RealTime
From Waiting click Next
From There click Back (to Here)

Escaping a threatening modern life
With the Goggles™ of an easy and safe
Virtual Life

Engrained

Engrained in the grind
forgetting it's the good things
that keep us alive.

Concentrating on entropy
forgetting it's the heat
that warms our lives.

Worried about time
forgetting it's the moments
that make up our lives.

Disturbed by the chaos
forgetting it's the journey
that is our lives.

The Road back to Verdun

May 1970

Verdun, July 2012

Verdun and The Somme

Verdun and The Somme
the two greatest horrors
mankind has ever inflicted
upon itself.

Verdun and The Somme
the closest man has descended
to creating hell on Earth
for himself.

Verdun and The Somme
and over a million men
die in the forts and trenches
by themselves.

Verdun and The Somme
and a hundred years passed
the memories are fading
despite themselves.

Verdun and The Somme
our hells to be remembered
lest we forget,
what's inside ourselves.

Verdun Now

An old battleground
not lost to the French.
Beyond living memory
for everyone else.

An old battlefield
a reminder of our failing.
Something to be remembered
the horrors we inflict
upon ourselves.

A century passes
and no-one actually remembers.
No-one who was there
is here anymore.

Sur le TGV again

Sur le TGV again
returning to Verdun.
Over forty years for me
and almost a hundred
since the battle was 'won'
[perhaps tactical victory better].

A high speed journey
returning through the years
to revisit childhood memories
that illuminated the horrors of war
still undimmed in the present day.

First night Verdun

First night Verdun
Shades of Bordeaux
Light on the Meuse
Imperial buildings glow
Then the heat fades
A dark blue sky appears
The street lights sparkle
The locals promenade
A few tourists linger
Music drifts down the Meuse
A quiet town comes to a close.

La Meuse

Walking through the woods

Walking through the woods
from the Museum to The Ossuaire.

Walking through the silence
from the rear to the frontline.

Walking through the heat
from the dark into the light.

Walking without birdsong
from butterflies at every step.

Walking with anticipation
to the greater silence ahead.

169

Verdun woods 2

Walking the Verdun woods
Silent woods
Shell-shocked woods
Paths pass monuments
Silent mounds
Amidst uneven ground
Only butterfly sound
Heard all around
Silent sounds
Nothing shall pass.

Men and mud

Bleeding white in the battle.
Of artillery never seen before.
Millions of shells shatter
the forests of Verdun.

And the men in the trenches and forts.
Where hundreds of thousands die.
Blown to pieces by the bombardment
reigning down from the sky.

Fort de Duamont

At the Ossuaire

At the Ossuaire the workmen toil
Erecting scaffolding all around
Preparing to clean years of grime
The cemeteries (too) cleansed above ground
Markers removed, crosses abound
Neat stacks mostly of markers lying on the ground
As the grass and flowers re-laid all around
Nothing disturbs the men below ground
Preparations made for century round
As no-one left remains above ground.

L.Ossuaire de Douaumont

Between their time and the future

A strange Ossuaire
Half bright and clean
Half dark dirty and old
A strange cemetery
Half old and tired
Half missing in renovation
A strange monument
Between the past and the present
Between yesterday and centenary
A strange vision
Between death and now
Between their time and the future

Le Tranchee des Baionettes

At the Tranchee des Baionnettes
the visitors arrive in their cars.
Park outside and walk fifty yards.
To a concrete rectangular blockhouse
shading those still inside from the sun.

Surprised by the lack of bayonets
they walk round it and are done.
Five minutes later back in the cars.
Leaving those forever entombed
alone in the ground.

Le Tranchee des Baionnettes

A Centenary approaches

A centenary approaches
and the graves need cleaned.
One hundred and thirty thousand
men in the ground
know nothing of this
resting so sound.

The new crosses are stacked
in piles at the side
while the grass is re-laid
and new flowers are found.
What do they care
the men in the ground.

They shall not pass

They shall not pass
Not now, here or evermore
Five soldiers in stone
A line never before
And then comes Maginot
La Defense never rests
Until La Patrie has passed
Old enemies become allies
And we forget the past.

'You shall not pass'
Monument to the children and motto of Verdun

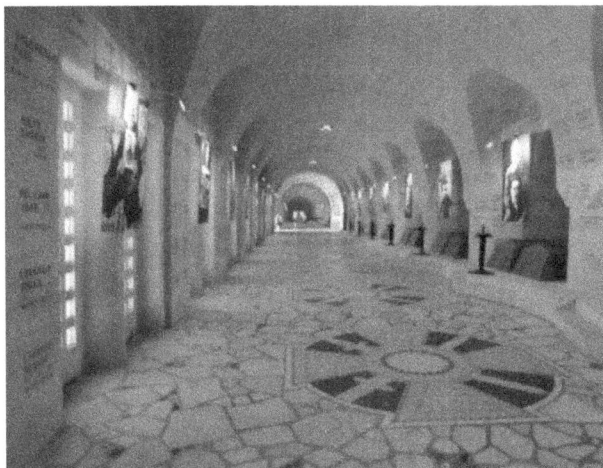

Inside the Ossuaire an orange light pervades.
All silent in awe of the sacrifice they made.
Every stone inscribed with a life lost.
Their bones beneath our feet
slowly turning to dust.

Fourth Stage Navigation

folding space and time
travelling through space and time
bringing back the space as time

AR: Augmented Reality

Overlays of information and connections
Overlays of people and voices.

Overlays of intelligence and adverts
Overlays of obscurity and cul-de-sacs.

Overlays of obvious and outlandish
Overlays of choice? and desire.

Overlays of decisions and dilemmas
Overlays of choice and chaos.

The Armies of Memory, and their Commander

An array of memories waiting for upload.
Waiting for programmes in machine code.

The armies of the network, and their controller.
A web of connections, waiting for data.
Waiting for commands and consequences.

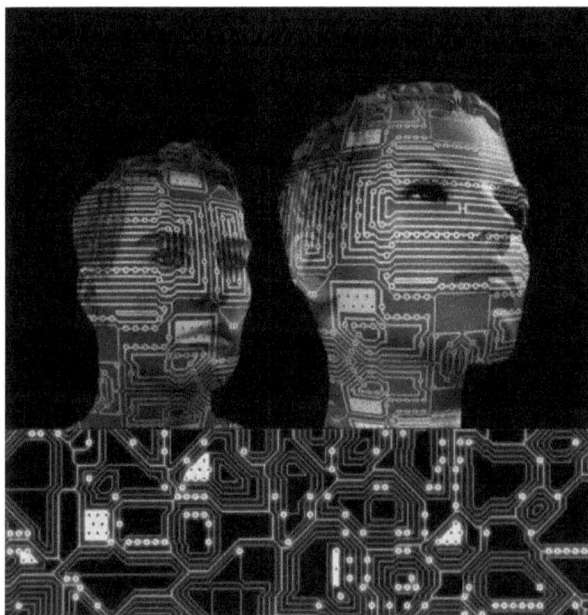

Backing-Up

Backing-Up
Backing-Up into a wall
Backing-Up into a stall
Backing-Up into a fall

Backing-Up into a commentary
Backing-Up into a story
Backing-Up into a memory

Modern times make man insecure
In a way no times have done before

Degrading information storage
Drawing the line
Drawing and redrawing the data
Information storage degrading

Information Degrades

A Darwinian Dead End
[The Immortality Conundrum]

Our genes are what make us.
But if the stem cells of our children
stolen from them
could give us immortality
and so no more children
need ever be born
and we lived on forever
this would be
our Darwinian dead end.

Haunted by Malthus

Malthus returns to haunt us
Carrying capacity exceeded
When unknown to us
Sustainable solutions recede
Imminent rebound taunts us
Die-back set to proceed.

Tidemarks

The tidemarks of dust
reach us every year
in our library of memories.

Washing back the past
a little less each year
our history turns to stories.

Out of time

Out of time all exits come
Every road runs out of time.

Out of time all ends are seen
Every path will reach an end.

Out of time we see the signs
Every moment is our now.

Colonia del Sacramento, Uruguay

Cephalonia, Greece

Botanical Gardens, Sydney

185

Looking for Zen Thrills

Not bungee-jumping
base jumping or any other
adrenalin based ing.
Mere primeval thrills
hardwired to the hindbrain.

Looking for frontal thrills
when calm appears from chaos.
From that still moment
Nature steps centre stage.
The Age of Reason proceeds.

'Lily' Leonardo da Vinci c1480

A New Dragon Year

An orchestra of ships and sirens
announce the New Year's arrival.

A dragon year starts and lies ahead of us.
Uncertain times, important times, thrilling times.

A year of new dragons never seen before.
Chaotic times, momentous times, changing times.

Doors closed, unknown till now
Doors open, unseen till now.

Chinese New Year, Singapore (2018)

Saving this spot

Saving this spot for myself
the grave-digger said
with a hint of a glint in his eye.

The best plot left I think
the grave-digger said
with a sigh and a glance of his eye.

You could book your plot now
the grave-digger said
with a smile and a twinkle in his eye.

That's a good idea I thought
think ahead the grave-digger said
with a knowing look visible in his eye.

The End of the Olympics

The End of the Olympics is in sight
when an athlete with artificial legs
competes alongside those with human legs.

The End of the Olympics is in sight
when one athlete with artificial legs
is faster than most with human legs.

The End of the Olympics is in sight
when all the athletes have artificial legs
and are all faster than those with human legs.

The End of the Olympics is in sight
when all the athletes have Nike or Adidas legs.
Then the competition is over
for those on human legs.

The Good Old Days

In the good old days
In the days of Empire and Raj
We were all just graveyard fodder
For those who ruled over us
And lived on the back
Of the toil of all our days
In those good old days.

6th Battalion Queens Own Cameron Highlanders, Battle of Loos, 26th September 1915 Joseph Gray © The Highlanders' Museum

Order and Disorder

Words
are life-support capsules for information.
Living forever now outside the mind.

Four thousand years later
first Morse then punched cards.
Then Turing machines
turned information
and everything into bits.

Erasing information
   uses energy
         increasing entropy.

[Landaur Limit –
      minimum energy needed
            to delete information.]

Distractions

Distractions
Buzzing insects in the brain
Distractions
Pestering thoughts of possible pain
Distractions
Nagging deeds needing done now
Distractions
Annoying actions waiting in the wings
Distractions
Tiresome chores calling their turn
Distractions
Relentless routines daily return
Distractions
Always, always demanding attention
Distractions
Do I have to go on?
Have you not got something better to do?

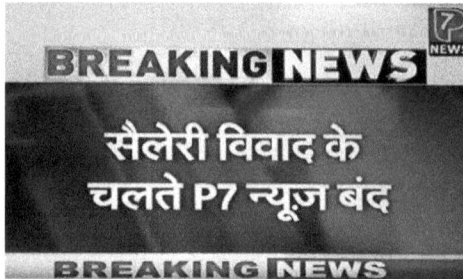

Tomorrow's news cycle

All tomorrow's papers
before I've gone to bed.

All tomorrow's news
before I've even slept.

Tomorrow's news now
breaking before you go.

Tomorrow's news cycle
won't let you go.

Rubbish Seagulls

The seagulls appear in the Spring
drawn from the nearby beaches
to the city's open and green spaces.

The sun-lovers appear in the Spring
drawn from the nearby boxes
to the city's open and green spaces.

The rubbish appears in the Spring
dropped from the thoughtless hands
all over the city's open and green spaces.

Waiting for lunch, Sydney Opera House Cafe

Virtual Life Lag

Fleeting meetings in the digital age
Short contacts in your digital life
All asynchronous in the digital world
No real connection in digital time
It's never now with digital communication
We do not share a digital moment
Always behind that digital divide
Real life is now, by your side.

On the quayside in Saint-Nazaire, France

Dunbar's Number

Suggested cognitive limit
to the number of people
with whom one can maintain
stable social relationships –
relationships in which an individual
knows who each person is
and how each person relates
to every other person.

First proposed in the 1990s
by British anthropologist Robin Dunbar,
who found a correlation between
primate brain size and average social group size.
By using the average human brain size
he calculated that humans can comfortably
maintain only 150 stable relationships.

Dunbar explained it informally as
"the number of people
you would not feel embarrassed
about joining uninvited
if you happened to bump into them in a bar".

Adapted from © Wikipedia, May 2018

More

New Neologisms

A net to catch the web

A net to catch the World Wide Web
A World Wide Wind of data
Sometimes with eyes
Sometimes with bots.

A net to catch the bots
A World Wide Weave of connections
Sometimes with vision
Sometimes with nets

A bot to catch the web
A World Wide Wave of visitors
Sometimes with memes
Sometimes with bot nets
Sometimes with web nets

TimeJolt

Wake up! All the alarms have started
the time to act has almost passed.

Wake up! The alarms have all stopped
the jolt to act has passed.

www.TimeJolt.com

next

MindedTo

Strike when the idea is still bold.
Acting that moment before it is old.

Strike before the idea gets cold.
Acting in advance of the moment being told.

www.MindedTo.com

previously

next

textexit

The penultimate one, only just begun.
Another sun, following every turn.

The ultimate one, now it must be done now with added fun.
Another text, following every exit.

www.textexit.com

previously

next

TimeDart

A pierced moment from the past,
flies through time designed to last.

A memory arrow from the past,
strikes through reality out with our grasp.

www.TimeDart.com

previously

next

ChaosFix

Closing the uncertainty with a final choice.
The decision chain ends and the loop is closed.

A high plateau of certainty all choices are possible.
This is the now moment when all nexts are possible.

www.ChaosFix.com

previously    **next**

FlatMeme

[The original point source of the growing idea.]

Moving forward through time
One heartbeat, one at a time.

One moment, each its own time
One present, always in time.

www.FlatMeme.com

previously

next

ZeroDees

Travelling to the corners
of a world growing smaller.

To meet an apparent stranger
with zero degrees of separation.

www.ZeroDees.com

previously   next

EmitTime

[Create a now between two moments.]

We have entangled ourselves together
Quantum events binding us together.

A strong force holds us together
In a dark matter universe together.

www.EmitTime.com

previously

next

digitock

Digital tracks leaving so much behind
making every step harder to find.

Digital memories we have all left behind
everything remains but can't be found.

www.digitock.com

previously

next

SoWhatSo

Grow up, get over it.
Move on to your new life.

So much better than the old life.
Happy to leave all that behind.

www.SoWhatSo.com

previously

fragments

Going to Gozo

It always begins with the first line.
Hunting for that moment, out of time.

Looking for words on paper
starting afresh again.
Looking for new words on paper
something fresh again.

This is my art

This is my art and this is me
what you get is what you see.
Don't ask me why this is me.

This is my art and this is me
what you see is what you get.
It's all of me and nothing yet.

Standing at the feet of giants
© Alison Boyd

Padrão dos Descobrimentos, *Monument to the Discoverers,*
on the Targus River at Belem near Lisbon.
It celebrates the Portuguese Age of Discovery in the 15th and 16th Century.
The figure at the apex is Henry the Navigator.

警告

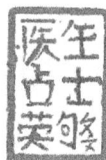

現在**不要**停
別抬頭
不要再聽

不要說話   別站著
不要問   **不要**採取行動
不要質疑   **不要**動

別看   **不要**這樣做
不要想像   **不要**那樣做
不明白   **不要**做任何事情

不覺得   **不要**做任何事
不要懷疑   現在**不要**做
不要拒絕   **不要**做任何事情

不要轉動   **不要**做任何事
別擔心   現在**不要**做
不要換   現在**不要**停止

Jamie Inglis is a poet and doctor from Edinburgh.

His poems are about travelling near and far, of times, places
and who we are. Poems about the unexpected and the
unexplained and about wars fought in our name.
Poems of new words embedded in the web.

He has worked and published on a wide range
of public health issues including HIV, cancer,
immunisation, tobacco, drugs and obesity.

He had his first poems published aged ten and after
qualifying in medicine returned to writing poetry
in the early 1980's.

His poems reflect his interests in people, pacifism,
politics, travel, science–fiction, the world we live in
and the world we are creating.

After travelling round the world five times
he still lives in Edinburgh.

发现
的道路

'Fisherman at Kajikazawa' Katsushika Hokusai

9 781916 354210

© **Prohibited** Publications
MMXX
www.prohibitedpublications.com

www.ingramcontent.com/pod-product-compliance
Lightning Source LLC
Chambersburg PA
CBHW072343090426
42741CB00012B/2906